GREAT IDEAS FOR GRANDKIDS!

GREAT IDEAS FOR GRANDKIDS!

150

Ways to
Entertain, Educate, and Enjoy
Your Grandchildren
Without Setting Foot
in a Toy Store!

Peggy Epstein

Contemporary Books

Chicago   New York   San Francisco   Lisbon   London   Madrid   Mexico City
Milan   New Delhi   San Juan   Seoul   Singapore   Sydney   Toronto

The **McGraw·Hill** Companies

Library of Congress Cataloging-in-Publication Data

Epstein, Peggy.
    Great ideas for grandkids! : 150 ways to entertain, educate, and enjoy your
grandkids without setting foot in a toy store / Peggy Epstein.
        p.   cm.
    ISBN 0-07-141191-7
    1. Grandparent and child.   2. Grandchildren—Psychology.   3. Creative
activities and seat work.   I. Title.

HQ759.9 .E67   2003
306.874'5—dc21   2002031417

1 2 3 4 5 6 7 8 9 0   LBM/LBM   2 1 0 9 8 7 6 5 4 3

ISBN 0-07-141191-7

McGraw-Hill books are available at special quantity discounts to use as premiums and
sales promotions, or for use in corporate training programs. For more information, please
write to the Director of Special Sales, Professional Publishing, McGraw-Hill, Two Penn
Plaza, New York, NY 10121-2298. Or contact your local bookstore.

This book is printed on acid-free paper.

For Cooper and his "Papa"

Contents

Introduction

The idea for this book came about after yet another exhausting expedition through a mega toy store. One so enormous and overwhelming and unfamiliar that it occurred to me someone in the travel industry should publish a guide for novices attempting to navigate its aisles.

Like many other grandparents I saw shopping that afternoon, I was on a quest for something just right for my grandchild. We naturally want to make our grandchildren happy, and it's the nature of our times to respond to that desire by giving them something, something they will really like.

What we really want, of course, is for our grandchildren to really like *us*, and for that liking to help build strong and meaningful relationships. Somewhere along the way, I realized an expensive trip to the toy store doesn't necessarily guarantee that end. That's when I started to stockpile a list of all kinds of activities grandparents and grandchildren can enjoy together.

So the point of this book is to offer help in changing the "what-did-you-bring-me?" syndrome into the "what-are-we-doing-today?" syndrome. The selection of activities was designed to provide lots of interaction between grandchild and grandparent, and lots of fun as well.

The activities were also designed to prove that it's possible to provide this fun for you and your grandchild without ever stepping into a toy store, and, in fact, without spending very much money at all. By saving much of what you would normally recycle, donate, or even throw away, you have the beginnings of your activity bin—a grocery carton, a laundry basket, or a closet shelf will do for this purpose. (Mine is a suitcase on wheels so I can take it along when we visit our grandchild.) And with a few extra items added to the grocery cart on your next trip to the supermarket, you're ready to go.

Question: Why would a kid who owns a state-of-the-art computer and a complete library of computer games want to play a game the two of you devised from a sponge and a paper cup? *Answer*: Because when you are listened to and taken seriously, praised and not criticized, given the gift of a grandparent's active participation, cheerful enthusiasm, and undivided attention—even if it's only for an hour—almost any activity becomes fun.

My own grandmother would have laughed at the idea of a book filled with ideas for having fun with your grandchild. And although the happiest hours of my childhood were spent with her, I never remember her buying me a toy. She did let me sprinkle on the coconut when she made strudel, tag along with her to the poultry market, eat bread and butter and nothing else, read aloud the stories I'd written, rock on the porch swing beside her on summer nights while she told me about the old country, and lie in bed beside her in the dark, asking her how to say words in Yiddish until I fell asleep.

When I was with her, I never doubted what her priority was.

So pick and choose among these activities, and look for the ones that will provide lots of fun—ones that will leave your grandchildren no doubt about your priorities.

Old-Fashioned Game Fun

Unlike today's enticing computer games and lavish board games, old-fashioned games are simple—but they are also flexible and forgiving. You get to make up the rules yourself, and you can change them whenever you want! The directions given for each game will provide you with a starting point.

Pitch It!

WHAT YOU'LL NEED

Crockery (take an expedition around the house looking for old candy dishes, ashtrays, teacups,
saucers, relish plates, etc.)
A package of dry lima beans
2 plastic sandwich bags
2 colored markers

PREPARATION

Using one of the markers, make a dot on both sides of fifteen beans. On another fifteen beans, make dots of a second color. Put each color of beans in its own sandwich bag.
Then make a big circle of crockery on the floor.

DIRECTIONS

Players stand in the middle of the circle. Each player is given
a bag of beans and takes turns pitching beans into the crock-

ery. The game ends when all of the beans have been thrown. Two points are awarded for each bean inside a dish; however, multiple beans in one dish count as only one point. *Variation*: allow three points for especially small dishes.

Note: You might tell your grandchild about the old-fashioned carnival game where people were invited to "step right up, toss your coins, and go home with a whole new set of dinnerware." Dishes were piled precariously high, and, like this game, landing a coin was harder than it looked!

Match It!

WHAT YOU'LL NEED

    16 paper cups
    2 each of 8 small items (such as pennies, paper clips, beans, etc.)
    Marker

<u>PREPARATION</u>

On the bottom of each cup, draw a different design, number, or letter of the alphabet. Place the small items on a table and cover each with a paper cup. Thoroughly scramble the cups by sliding them around on the table.

<u>DIRECTIONS</u>

Player number one picks up a cup, looks at the item underneath, and replaces the cup. The same player then looks under another cup; if the items match, the player keeps the items. Play continues until all of the matches are made. The player with the most pairs of matching items wins.

Note: Make the game tougher! Use 24 cups and 12 objects, or use three like objects instead of two. Older kids will enjoy playing the game without the clues drawn on the cups.

Catch It!

WHAT YOU'LL NEED

An empty oatmeal box or coffee can
Wrapping paper and tape
Kitchen sponge and scissors

PREPARATION

Cover the box or can with wrapping paper (just for decoration). Cut the sponge into three-inch squares.

DIRECTIONS

Toss a sponge square into the air and try to catch it with the container. Try two. Try three! For a grandchild/grandparent competition, keep track of how many sponges you each catch. For a two-person variation, use two containers and try to catch the sponge when it's tossed out of the opponent's container.

Note: For older kids use smaller cans and smaller pieces of sponge. For a real challenge, use a tomato paste can and a *minuscule* piece of sponge.

That's the Last Straw!

<u>WHAT YOU'LL NEED</u>
30 toothpicks

<u>PREPARATION</u>
Place the toothpicks on a table in three piles. It doesn't matter how many toothpicks are in each pile.

<u>DIRECTIONS</u>
Players take turns removing toothpicks from the piles. You can remove any number you like, but you may only take from one pile on each turn. The object of the game is to be

the player who picks up the last toothpick. It's trickier than it sounds!

Note: This game used to be played with broom straws (before someone decided this was an unsanitary practice). You might like to explain this to your grandchild, as well as how the expression "that's the last straw" (the one that broke the camel's back) is used today.

Alphabet in My Suitcase
(a good in-the-car activity)

DIRECTIONS

The first person begins: "I packed my suitcase for Hawaii (or anywhere you would both like to travel) and in it I took an *alligator*."

The second person picks up the story: "I packed my suitcase for Hawaii and in it I took an *alligator* and a *brick*."

The game continues through the rest of the alphabet with players remembering the previously mentioned objects, repeating them in alphabetical order, and adding a new object to the list.

Note: For younger children, instead of the alphabet use the numbers one through ten. "I put one teddy bear in my suitcase." "I put one teddy bear and two cookies in my suitcase." Older children can enhance the game with adjectives: "an agitated alligator, a broken brick," and so on.

Dots

WHAT YOU'LL NEED

Unlined paper

Pencils or pens of two different colors

PREPARATION

Draw a line of eight evenly spaced dots across the top of the paper. Drop down a little space, and make eight more dots, making sure each dot lines up with the one above it.

DIRECTIONS

Players take turns making one straight line between two dots. Every time you make the fourth line to complete a square, place your initial inside the square and take an extra turn. When the whole paper has been turned into squares, count to see who has the most!

Three Hiding Games

Hide-and-Seek

In the traditional version of this game, players take turns hiding and finding each other, but to add interest you might want to have seekers count to 100 by two's or four's, or you might want to set some exact perimeters (the basement is a no-hide zone, for example).

Note: Keep in mind that small children often enjoy hiding (and having you hide) in exactly the same place. Very little children sometimes believe themselves to be invisible if their eyes are closed. Older children sometimes like to use a timer.

Hotter! Colder!
Players take turns hiding an object such as a ball. The hider of the object calls out clues to the finder by yelling out various degrees of "hot" and "cold." Players who get stuck at "freezing!" could be helped with a few directional clues.

Ten Pennies
This game works best when played in a small room. The hider may hide any number of pennies up to ten. The hider keeps any pennies not hidden in tightly clenched fists. A

timer is activated as the finder begins to look. When the time is up, OR when the finder claims to have found all of the hidden pennies, those pennies are counted. If the finder has found all ten pennies OR if the finder has found the number of pennies hidden, the finder receives ten points. *Be warned*: Some kids get a kick out of hiding no pennies at all; it's lots of fun to sit back and watch you search!

King O'Clock Solitaire

WHAT YOU'LL NEED

A deck of cards (two decks for a competition)

PREPARATION

Shuffle the cards. Make thirteen piles of four cards each. Arrange the piles on the floor like a big clock with one stack in the middle.

<u>DIRECTIONS</u>

Explain that each number should be placed in its hour position, the Jack goes in the 11:00 position, the Queen is 12:00, and the King goes in the middle. The object of the game is to get all the cards in their correct piles before all four Kings show up in the middle. Start at the 1:00 pile. Turn over the top card and put it where it goes. For example, if the first card turned over is a seven, put it face up under the 7:00 pile. Then take the top card from the 7:00 pile and put it wherever it goes. You lose if the fourth King shows up before your clock is finished.

Note: A second player can "assist" the solitaire player or can play with a separate deck for a "beat the clock" race.

Simon Says (with variations)

You and your grandchild can take turns being Simon in these two-person versions.

Basic game (great for small children)

The leader—called Simon—tells the follower what to do. For example, Simon might say, "Touch your toes" or "Clap your hands." However, the follower should only follow directions when the leader says, "*Simon says* touch your toes." Using props adds to the fun (putting on a hat, stepping over a book, etc.).

Advanced Game

Three directions are given at once. ("Simon says look down, scratch your ear, and put your hand on your hip.")

Really Advanced Game

Simon says, "Do the opposite" or "Do the same." For example: "Simon says touch your left foot—same" and the follower follows the directions, or "Simon says, rub your tummy and pat your head—opposite" and the follower must do the opposite.

Feel It, Find It

WHAT YOU'LL NEED
    2 paper lunch sacks
    2 each of various objects such as sponge cubes, jar
        lids, buttons, tiny balls, nuts, erasers, etc.

PREPARATION
Put identical objects in each sack.

DIRECTIONS
Without looking, the first player pulls an object out of his or
her sack. The second player must fish out the same object
without looking. If incorrect, the second player must put the
object back. Then the second player takes out an object for
the first player to match. The first player with an empty sack
is the winner.

Note: For very young children, use four or five easily differentiated objects. Older kids will like trying to make finer distinctions; for example, you might use pennies, dimes, different sizes of washers, buttons, round game pieces.

Boxed-In

<u>WHAT YOU'LL NEED</u>
Paper and pencil

<u>DIRECTIONS</u>
The first player thinks of a word and writes a space for each letter on the paper. For example: ___ ___ ___ ___ ___ ___ (the word is "monkey"). The game proceeds as follows: The guesser guesses the letter *E*. The first player writes the letter

E in the appropriate place. (If the word contained two *E*s, both would be written in at the same time.) The guesser guesses the letter *P*, but there is no *P* in the word, so the first player draws the round head of a stick figure.

Game continues. If the stick figure is finished and boxed-in (a head, a body, two arms, two legs, and a four-sided box around it) before the guesser guesses the word, the guesser loses.

Note: As you may have noticed, this is actually the game of "Hangman," but the name has been changed in the spirit of fun.

Sandwich

WHAT YOU'LL NEED

Deck of cards (the suits are irrelevant in this game)

<u>PREPARATION</u>

Divide cards into two even stacks placed facedown in front of two players.

<u>DIRECTIONS</u>

Players each put one card face*up* on the table. The player with the higher card takes both cards. If the cards are alike (for example, two Jacks), the players make a sandwich. This means they each put another card face*down* on top of the first card. Then they put another card face*up* on the top of the pile. The player with the higher card takes both "sandwiches." If the two cards are alike again, players make double-decker sandwiches and continue as before. The game is over when one player has all the cards.

Note: This game was originally known as "War."

Make Your Own
Tic-Tac-Toe

WHAT YOU'LL NEED

A variety of materials that might include, but are certainly not limited to, the following: cardboard from grocery cartons, leftover carpet or tile squares, colored papers, buttons, spools, washers, nuts, bottle tops, magazine illustrations, and so on.

DIRECTIONS

By using your imaginations, you and your grandchild can give new life to a classic game. For example, make a tiny tic-tac-toe set from a leftover ceramic tile and two colors of buttons; then make an enormous one for the backyard from an old plastic tablecloth and two-liter soda pop bottles filled with two colors of water.

Cooking Fun

Cooking fun counts twice—once for the fun of creating and once for the fun of eating together. Since children are naturally finicky beings, you might want to present these activities as opportunities to create. If your grandchild wants to sample the finished product, terrific! If not, your line is "Thanks for helping me make something I'm definitely going to enjoy eating!"

Lots of sweets are included here, of course, but there are also ideas for "real food" kids just might go for.

Instant Pudding
(from a box)

Having boxes of instant pudding on hand makes for quick preparation of a tasty treat children and grandparents can easily prepare together. For added fun, try these variations:

- Layer two different flavors for a parfait
- Serve in an ice-cream cone
- Line up a buffet of toppings: granola, raisins, chocolate chips, chopped peanuts, crushed pineapple, sliced bananas, maraschino cherries, etc.
- Spread between graham crackers

Instant Pudding
(made from scratch)

WHAT YOU'LL NEED

2 ripe bananas
½ cup applesauce
2 tablespoons peanut butter
2 tablespoons honey
Cinnamon

DIRECTIONS

Mash bananas well in a large bowl. Add applesauce, peanut butter, and honey, stirring after each addition. Serve in two small bowls. Sprinkle with as much cinnamon as you like.

Edible Candles
(including the fire!)

WHAT YOU'LL NEED
> Lettuce leaves
> Canned pineapple, in rings
> Bananas
> Jelly or jam
> Maraschino cherries

DIRECTIONS
Wash and dry the lettuce leaves, then place each leaf on a small dish. Open the pineapple, drain it well, and place one slice of pineapple on each lettuce leaf. Next, peel the bananas and cut off the ends to make a nice straight piece of banana. Finally, cut a piece of maraschino cherry so that it looks like a flame. To assemble the candle (in its holder), put a little jam inside the hole of the pineapple, set the

banana in the hole, put a little jam on top of the candle, and stand the cherry on top of the banana candle. Serve and eat!

Pizza!
(two versions)

Pizza for Dinner

For an easy pizza crust, use packaged English muffins or plain bagels, split open and spread with prepared pizza sauce. Garnish with any or all of the following: shredded cheese, olives, cooked and crumbled hamburger or sausage, chopped or sautéed green peppers, onions, mushrooms, crushed pineapple, and so on.

Pizza for Dessert

Open a tube of refrigerated cookie dough and roll it into a large pizza-sized circle on a greased cookie sheet. Decorate with any of the following: chocolate chips, candy sprinkles, nuts, coconut, maraschino cherries, raisins, or your favorite candy. Bake according to package directions. Cut into wedge-shaped pieces and serve while still warm.

Bring Those Rarely Used Kitchen Items Out of Hiding

Fondue Pot

Dipping pound cake squares and banana pieces into melted chocolate is always a winner, but chunks of French bread dipped into melted cheese might go over in a big way. Here's a recipe tailored to kids' tastes.

<u>WHAT YOU'LL NEED</u>

    1 can (1⅔ cups) unsweetened condensed milk
    Salt and pepper
    2 cups grated cheese (American or Cheddar)
    1 tablespoon cornstarch
    French or Italian bread, cut into chunks

<u>DIRECTIONS</u>

Place the milk in a bowl and warm it in the microwave; stir in a little salt and pepper. Mix the grated cheese with the cornstarch, then slowly add the cheese to the hot milk, stirring well. Put the cheese and milk mixture into the fondue pot and cook a little longer. Put a chunk of bread on a fondue fork, dip into sauce, and enjoy.

Doughnut Maker

They're messy—but probably worth at least a one-time adventure. Kids like garnishing plain cake doughnuts by dipping them into icing and then into coconut, chopped nuts, or candy sprinkles.

Spritz Cookie Press
They're just like Play-doh machines with tastier results! Try two colors of dough forced through the press side by side.

Slow Cooker
Starting a stew or soup in the morning and checking on it every hour or two provides entertainment for grandchildren—and dinner at the end of the day. Kids can help cut vegetables, pour in liquids, add seasonings, or do other small tasks.

Bread Making Machine
Making bread from scratch is a great all-day activity if you have the inclination, but bread making machines can provide excellent results with a much smaller time—and work—commitment.

Another idea: Buy frozen bread dough. Thaw, and let kids shape small loaves to their liking.

Ice Cream Maker

Try inventing unique flavors. For example, cooked carrots added to a vanilla ice cream recipe (minus the vanilla flavoring and plus some nutmeg) makes a tasty and nutritional treat.

Grandma's (or ˜pa's) Granola

WHAT YOU'LL NEED

> 4 cups uncooked oatmeal
> 1–2 cups wheat germ
> Cinnamon, nutmeg, or other flavorings
> Orange juice
> Honey
> Slivered almonds (optional)
> Raisins or other dried fruit (optional)

DIRECTIONS

Preheat oven to 350 degrees. Mix the first five ingredients together in a large bowl. Adjust the amount of orange juice and honey to match how much sweetness you want. You're aiming for a "stick-together" texture. Spread the ingredients out on two large cookie sheets with sides, bake for half an hour, stirring every ten minutes.

Turn the oven down to 200 degrees and warm the granola in the oven for a couple of hours until it's toasty and dry. Remove the granola and mix with nuts and dried fruit. Store in tightly covered containers or plastic storage bags.

Note: This recipe makes a big batch. You might want to make only half, but kids will enjoy packaging granola in jars they've washed and dried, adding a handmade label, tying a ribbon around the neck of the jar, and giving as presents to family and friends.

Orange Marmalade

This is another easy-to-prepare gift item the two of you can make together.

<u>WHAT YOU'LL NEED</u>
>   Oranges
>   Sugar

<u>DIRECTIONS</u>
Cut up the unpeeled orange and shred it in a food processor. Measure to find out how much orange you have, and then measure out the same amount of sugar. Put the orange and sugar into a glass bowl. Cook the mixture in the microwave, stirring once a minute for about five minutes or until the mixture thickens. Cover and store in the refrigerator.

Note: If making marmalade for gifts, kids can wash out small jars, dry thoroughly, and make colorful labels (orange "balls" and green leaves) with a reminder that marmalade should be refrigerated.

Peanut Power

Making Peanut Butter

Probably the only reason for making this inexpensive, easy-to-find commodity is that kids get a kick out of the process. Here's a simple recipe for Chunky Peanut Butter using only peanuts—buy them unshelled so kids can have the fun of shelling them before you start on the recipe.

DIRECTIONS

Put half of the peanuts in a food processor and grind until the peanuts have turned into little chunks. Remove from the processor. Put in the other half of the peanuts and grind until they are thoroughly pureed. By hand, mix the two batches together.

What's for Dinner? Peanut Butter!

Since peanut butter is such a childhood treasure, it ought to be used with more than just jelly. You and your grandchild will have fun making—and eating—this peanut butter inspired dinner.

For the main course, thread strips of boneless chicken breasts onto skewers. Bake or grill until done. (If grilling, be sure to soak wooden skewers beforehand.) Serve the chicken kabobs with a spicy dipping sauce made from peanut butter thinned with a little ketchup, soy sauce, honey, and garlic powder to taste.

Make peanut butter muffins to go with the kabobs by stirring a small amount of peanut butter into a boxed apple muffin mix. Celery, stuffed with you-know-what, will also make a great side dish.

For dessert, serve the made-from-scratch instant pudding found at the beginning of this chapter.

Stuff It!

Stuff It: Suit Yourself

Kids enjoy preparing wraps when they can select their own fillings. Provide a "wrapper" (such as a tortilla or a pancake) and let kids decide what to stuff inside. Here are some possibilities: scrambled or chopped hard-boiled eggs, cubed chicken, slivered ham, shredded cheese, chopped carrots, tomatoes, or other vegetables.

Stuff It: Ethnic Style

Here's an idea for introducing your grandchild to some ethnic foods. You might point out that all of the following are really just variations of rolling and stuffing: egg rolls, blintzes, manicotti, crepes, tamales, and gyros, to name a few. Look up some recipes and try them out, tailoring the ingredients to your grandchild's taste. Or, if you have the opportunity, sample some of these foods at ethnic festivals.

Artichoke
(Yeah, you can actually eat this thing!)

Because they look so incredibly inedible, some kids really get into the challenge of cooking artichokes. Here's an easy way to prepare them:

❶ Pick off the small outer leaves near the stem. ❷ Cut the stem off flush with the bottom of the artichoke. ❸ Place artichoke in a large pot of lightly salted boiling water for 40 to 60 minutes (depending on size). ❹ Remove the artichoke with tongs and drain upside down.

The artichokes can be served hot or cold, but room temperature probably works best for kids. Be sure to show your grandchildren how to remove the leaves and scrape them against their teeth. Leaves can be dipped in mayonnaise or melted butter if desired.

Note: It takes practice to cut out the heart of the artichoke, so this is probably a grandparent job.

Pasta Toss

Keeping boxed macaroni and cheese dinners on hand is always a good idea, but here's another pasta possibility.

Choose an interesting-looking pasta and boil until done. (You could even combine small amounts of various leftover pastas.) While the pasta is cooking, prepare the ingredients you would like in your pasta toss. Here are a few ideas: Parmesan cheese, grated mozzarella cheese, little cubes of meats or poultry, olives, tiny canned shrimp, vegetable chunks (such as tomatoes, mushrooms, or green peppers). Once the pasta is done, drain it thoroughly and toss with a little olive oil and any of the above ingredients. Add extra seasonings or herbs for a more grown-up taste.

Two Corny Ideas

Corn on the Cob

If you can find corn with the husks still on, you can make an activity out of getting the corn stripped and ready for the pot. Kids especially like to eat corn when it's been broken into thirds or even fourths and speared with corn holders. Or you can impale the whole cob, ice cream bar style, onto a sturdy skewer. It's also fun to grill corn in their husks on an outdoor grill.

Corn Muffins

When you're both in the mood to bake, but you think your grandchild is sugared out, try corn muffins. Most recipes only contain a tablespoonful of sugar for an entire batch of muffins, and even boxed corn mixes have a low sugar count.

Teach Your Grandchild to Fly Solo in the Kitchen

When grandchildren are old enough, most will enjoy the wonderful feeling that comes from knowing they can cook an entire meal all by themselves.

Start by leafing through cookbooks together or browsing Internet sites to find a perfect menu—one that is not too difficult to prepare but is suitable for a company meal.

Teach your grandchild to make only one part of the dinner at a time. For example, try baked chicken one day. Show how to make potato salad another time. Do a fruit salad on a third day. (These can all be incorporated into whatever else you happen to be serving for that night's meal.) Then hold a practice run: with you in the next room, allow your grandchild to cook the complete meal independently. Resist the urge to peek in or even shout out "May I help?" If you're needed, you'll be called for.

After a successful practice run, offer the use of your best dishes and allow your grandchild to choose the dinner guests for the real thing.

Share Your Specialty

Perhaps you're known for some culinary treat? Share your "secret" recipe with your grandchild. Make a handwritten copy of the recipe on a special card or sheet of paper. With practice and encouragement, young teenagers might be able to proudly take over the preparation of your specialty for family gatherings, and even a four-year-old can assist you with the measuring and mixing.

Collecting Fun

Kids have a natural mania for collecting. Toy manufacturers and media marketers capitalize on this mania with fast-food give-aways and seemingly endless add-ons to those action toy series or fashion doll wardrobes.

For a different kind of collecting, your grandchild might like to try some of the following no-cost collections. You can help get the collection going, and the two of you can work on it together whenever you have the chance. Although you might want to collaborate on building the collection, your greatest contribution will likely be your willingness to be an enthusiastic admirer when your young collector wants you to look over the collection for the umpteenth time.

Collect Signs

The two of you might have fun collecting signs, especially if you spend time in the car together. You won't be collecting the actual signs, of course, but you'll keep a record of the signs you see. This is a great activity to prevent long car rides from becoming boring. First, decide on a theme for your collection, such as unusual traffic signs or signs advertising restaurants. Quickly jot down the words you see on a sign first, and then make a note of its shape and color later. You might like to see how many funny ones you can find. If you have a camera, you can make a photographic collection of the signs you have seen.

Collect Place Names

If you're both interested in geography, this is a collection you can work on from time to time when you're together. Start by picking a theme, something like places with animal names (Beaver, Buffalo, and Lone Wolf, for example, are all towns in Oklahoma). Use an atlas as your resource and a notebook to record the names, adding illustrations if you like. If you have a large map, you could mark the names in your collection with colorful dots or pins. Other themes for name-collecting might include places with flower, famous people, or color names.

Collect Comic Strips

Find a grandchild-appropriate cartoon strip in the daily newspaper. You can cut out the strip each day, paste it onto one page in a notebook, and read from the notebook when your grandchild comes to visit. Your grandchild can then add comments like "This is a really funny one!" or "I knew he'd get in trouble with those scissors." Kids might like to decorate the pages with drawings of the cartoon characters.

Collect Pencils and Pens

Start by looking around both of your houses for interesting pens and pencils. Ask family members and neighbors if they can make any contributions to your collection. Whenever either of you visits a business—a bank, for example—mention your collection and ask if they might donate a pen or pencil. Cover empty soup cans with attractive wrapping paper to create holders for displaying various categories of your collection.

Collect Recipes

A grandparent/grandchild recipe collection could fall into several categories, including

- *Our Family's Favorite Recipes.* Ask family members to furnish these along with a little comment on why it's a favorite. Paste them into a decorated notebook.
- *Recipes We Would Like to Try.* File these away for future cooking adventures.
- *Recipes from Famous People.* You can often find these in cookbooks available at the library or on the Internet, or you might even try writing to famous people and requesting their favorite recipes.
- *Recipes for Non-Food Items.* Try finding recipes for homemade soap bubbles, play-clay, glass cleaner, dog biscuits, and so on.

Collect Menus

Collect menus from restaurants whenever you eat out (restaurants will often give them to you if you explain that you're a collector). Both grandparents and grandchildren could ask friends and relatives to bring home menus as souvenirs when they visit other cities. Don't forget the take-out menus you might find on the counters of fast-food places. Grandchildren could contribute their school cafeteria menus to the collection. Each of you might like to write a fantasy menu for one perfect meal, or even an entire menu for an imaginary restaurant.

Collect Greeting Cards

Grandparents will probably have a start for this collection already, but neither of you will have much trouble convincing your friends, relatives, and neighbors to save their old cards for you. No one ever really knows what to do with them, and they mount up quickly.

Once you've filled a good-sized box, decide what kind of collection it will be and start sorting them. Kids might like to collect only cards with pictures of animals, for example. Funny cards also make a good collection.

You can even use parts of the cards to make new cards (see the Creative Fun chapter).

Collect Riddles

If your grandchild likes jokes, a riddle collection can be lots of fun. Encourage your young riddler to carry around a tiny notebook for jotting down new ones. A good strategy is to write the riddle on the front of the page and the answer on the back. What are good resources for riddles? In addition to their own friends, encourage grandkids to ask your friends if they can remember riddles from their childhood. The children's section of the library always stocks books filled with riddles.

Here's a nice riddle-inspired gift for a friend who needs cheering up: Write each of your riddles on a strip of brightly colored paper and put the answer on the back. Use scissors to "curl" the strip. Put all of the curly strips into an empty glass jar. Tie a ribbon around the top of the jar, and add a card that reads, "Take as needed for laughs."

Collect Signatures

An easy-to-accumulate collection for both of you is a signature collection. Ask people you know to write their signatures on a 3″ × 5″ card. You and your grandchild will be amazed by how differently people sign their names. (If the signature is really hard to read, print the name on the back before you forget to whom it belongs!) File your cards in a recipe box in alphabetical order.

You might like to check out a book from the library on handwriting analysis; it may not be scientific, but it's lots of fun. While you're at the library, you can look up (with the librarian's help) the addresses of your favorite celebrities. Then send them a card to sign. For more information, see the chapter on Writing Fun.

Collect Broken Appliances

Why, you might ask? Because taking stuff apart can be enormously satisfying for both grandchild and grandparent. Ask your family and neighbors to hand over those old clocks and toasters instead of tossing them into the trash bin. Make sure you cut off all of the electrical cords before you begin. As you take things apart, use cans, jars, and boxes to sort the different "parts" you come across. The two of you may enjoy this simple taking-apart activity, or you could use the parts to make something else—a mobile or a friendly robot statue, for example.

Collect Rocks

Start your collection by looking for rocks in your neighborhood and your grandchild's neighborhood. If either of you go on a vacation, try to find a few rocks. You might ask friends and family members to bring back a stone or two from places they travel. The more rocks you collect, the more differences you will see. If the two of you want to know more, books from the library can offer a wealth of information about the different types of rocks.

A good place to store them is an egg carton, where each specimen can have its own spot. Cut off the tops of the egg cartons if you have a large space to display your collection. Otherwise, close the tops and stack up the cartons.

Collect Children's Books
(to give away)

Family shelters, hospitals, and even dentists' offices are places where nervous children might be helped by looking at picture books. Encourage your grandchildren to go through their own collections, looking for books they no longer read. Then you can tell your family, friends, and neighbors about your collection and ask for donations. Collect books that are unmarked and clean; you can wipe dusty covers off with a damp paper towel and dry carefully. If a book has a few small marks, cover them with brightly colored stickers. When you have a small boxful, make a trip together to deliver the books.

Collect Glass Bottles

Look for bottles with interesting shapes such as the kind oil or vinegar might come in. Wash them thoroughly. You might want to paint the lids with silver or gold paint. Then fill the bottles with water and add a tiny bit of food coloring to each one. Display them in a sunny window or outside on a porch.

Collect "Paper Stuff" About a Favorite Food

This is a silly but entertaining collection you can work on together from time to time. First, choose a common food you both especially like. This might be pizza, potatoes, sandwiches, or ice cream. You will want to keep your collection in a scrapbook. If you can't find an old one, make a new scrapbook using construction paper and cardboard. Punch holes in the construction paper and cardboard and lace them together with a shoestring. Decorate the cardboard cover with pizza coupons, magazine photos of ice cream treats, or any other paper image of your chosen food.

Next make a title page: "The Perfect Potato" or "I Scream for Ice Cream" or "Pizza Pizzazz," for example. Now, what will go in your scrapbook? You can paste in advertisements and recipes. You can find your food's history and records (what was the largest sandwich ever made?), you can list family members' or friends' favorite kinds of pizza, you can find out if there are any riddles or jokes about your favorite food, you can draw potato people or enormous ice cream sundaes. You and your grandchild can even work together to write a story or poem about your favorite treat. Be imaginative and have fun filling up the pages!

Collect Maps

Find a large box and an old road map. Cover the box with the map, gluing down the edges firmly. Use a marker to write "Map Collection" on the top of the box. Then start looking for your maps.

- Check the newspaper for maps of places in the news.
- Ask family members and neighbors for maps they no longer use.
- Print some maps from the Internet. Also, while you are online, check for state tourist organizations that will mail you free maps.
- At the library, photocopy interesting maps.
- Try drawing maps. Go for a walk and then draw a map of your grandchild's neighborhood along with a map of your neighborhood.

Reading Fun

Even the tiniest child enjoys snuggling in a lap and sharing a story, and even if you're a long-distance grandparent, you can share this experience by mailing audio or videotapes on which you've recorded stories for your grandchild.

But as a child grows older, there are many more challenging and entertaining ways for grandparents and grandchildren to share the pleasure of books and reading. *One note*: even if you're eager to show your enthusiasm over a young reader's skills, remember that kids usually prefer to read aloud when it's their own choice, so it's best to wait and let them volunteer.

Alphabet Mat

Fun for the littlest "readers." An old sheet or vinyl tablecloth (a sheet-sized piece of white oilcloth would be even better) can be made into a great alphabet mat. Divide the mat into squares using a yardstick and a permanent marker. Inside each square, draw a large block letter. You might fill in the letters with stripes or dots of varying colors. You can arrange the letters in alphabetical order or follow the order on a computer keyboard.

As a child begins to learn the alphabet, you can play a simple game such as "Let me see you stand on the *B*. Now sit on the *Q* and jump on the *M*." Later, the child might find household objects to match up with various squares (a pencil on *P*, for example).

An older child might enjoy helping you make an alphabet mat for a younger sibling or cousin.

Note: Your grandchild might find other uses for the alphabet mat: rolling up in it, throwing it over a chair for a tent, driving toy cars around it, and so on. Show your appreciation for such ingenuity!

Read What They're Reading

Once kids have progressed from the picture book to the chapter book phase, ask their parents for the names of books your grandchildren are currently reading. Spend some time with those books at the library or the bookstore. By doing so, you'll gain a whole new area of connection with your grandchild. You can have hours of fun talking with your grandchild about the exploits of the characters in these books, the funny things that happen, the surprise endings, or what might happen in the next book.

Share What You're Reading

When appropriate, show your grandchild a book you're currently reading. Give a simplified version of the plot. Describe the characters. Predict what you think will happen. Keep your grandchild posted on further developments.

Read Reviews

Locate reviews the two of you would enjoy reading together. Look for them in newspapers, magazines, and various websites. Your librarian can direct you to reviews of children's books. Point out that many reviews have two parts: the first part usually gives a general overview and is more objective; the second part often gives the reviewer's opinion. If you have read the book, ask yourselves if anything you consider important was left out of the review.

Decide whether you agree or disagree with the reviewer's point of view.

Become Experts

Select a rare animal, a little-known scientist, an obsolete car, or another somewhat obscure topic. Working together, use encyclopedias, online resources, material from the library, and other methods of research to find out everything you can about your chosen subject. If possible, try to locate a primary source. For example, a herpetologist at a zoo in your community might be willing to talk to you and your grandchild about a particular snake, or a member of a local car club would probably be happy to fan your interest in the car he drove as a teenager. A bonus feature of this activity is the complete awe your knowledge on this subject will elicit when the two of you discuss your newly acquired information at the next family gathering.

Enjoy the Newspaper Together

The daily paper is full of treasures for kids. Sure, the comic strips come immediately to mind, but not all of them are actually kid-appropriate. If you find a suitable comic your grandchild enjoys, however, you might like to clip, share, and even save the best strips. (See the Collecting Fun chapter.)

Other ideas for using the newspaper:

- For kids who are interested, "read" the newspaper together by looking at the photos and discussing what's happening in them.
- Search the paper for the hero of the day. Discuss a person who has done something worthwhile and made a difference in the lives of others.
- Find and read good news articles about kids and/or animals.
- Follow the stats of a favorite sports team. Cut out articles about a favorite player. (Writing a letter to

that player is another idea; for suggestions, look in the chapter on Writing Fun.)

- Read the classified ads together. What have people lost? How much do people get paid to drive trucks? Where can you take ballet lessons? What dog would you buy?
- Explain that horoscopes are just for fun and then read them for that.
- With older kids, you can read an appropriate question to Dear Abby, and then compare the advice each of you would give to the writer. After that, read the columnist's response and discuss.

From the Library

Trips to the library are fun for kids who don't already go on a regular basis. But using the library yourself before a grandchild's visit can arm you with hours of ready-to-go fun. Check out some of these books to have on hand during the visit:

- Books of three-minute mysteries
- Books of riddles and jokes
- Books featuring simple magic tricks (be sure to gather the needed supplies)
- Books of world records and amazing feats
- Books of folktales from different countries
- Books of modern short poems
- Books showing optical illusions
- Books that show how to make shadow pictures
- Books that list names and their meanings
- Books on the subject of your grandchild's current fascination (bugs, rockets, ice skating, etc.). The librarian can help you locate the children's subject index to *Books in Print*, which will lead you to titles of appropriate books.

Read the Classics—on TV!

While you're at the library, think about a classic book you hope your grandchild will read some day and check out the movie version. Tell your grandchild why the book made such an impression on you. Make a big batch of popcorn and watch the film together. Seeing a movie made from the classic tale just might spur your young reader into asking for the print version. Ideas include *To Kill a Mockingbird*, *David Copperfield*, *Tom Sawyer*, *A Journey to the Center of the Earth*, *The Adventures of Robin Hood*, and *Little Women*.

Guess Mess

Guessing is not only fun, it's also a great thinking strategy that can improve reading comprehension. Try this idea in two ways:

- When reading aloud a new picture book, ask your grandchild to guess what will happen before you turn the page. If necessary, you could give clues. Cheer for correct guesses and give positive reinforcement for others: "Well, your idea was a good one, too."

- When reading a book that's familiar to your grandchild, *you* make the guesses before turning the page. Explain the logic behind your serious guesses, but also offer a few outrageous ones. Kids love to point out when you're totally messing up the story!

Make Bookmarks for Each Other

Simply clip off a big corner from a used envelope; you will have a double triangle with an opening just perfect for marking your page. Decorate these with markers or crayons and then exchange your new bookmarks.

Storeroom Stories

WHAT YOU'LL NEED

A box filled with little pictures you've clipped from
    magazines—this box will be the "storeroom."
Paper and pen
Paste or glue

PREPARATION

Explain that the two of you are going to make up a story,
but the pictures are already drawn. Invite the child to look
through the storeroom.

DIRECTIONS

Begin the story with the traditional "Once upon a time there
was a . . ." Write the words out on a large sheet of paper (or
be prepared to use many sheets since the pictures will take
up a lot of space). Then ask the child to choose a picture
from the storeroom and paste it at the end of the sentence.

Continue the story by letting the child select pictures. For example: "One day the girl came home from school and saw a (picture goes here)." Work together to continue the story line. Once you are finished, read the (probably silly) story together, letting the child say the name of the pictures as you come to them.

Learn a Poem Together

Read through the poems in a child's book of simple rhyming verse. Select something short you both like. Talk about the steps involved in memorizing, such as making pictures in your mind and learning one line at a time. You could then recite your poem in unison at your next family gathering.

For very young children, you might create your own poem for them to memorize. For example: "In spring, I sing" or "I like my trike."(Sure, these are poems!)

And speaking of poems . . .

Share a Classic
Narrative Poem

You might remember learning a "story poem" in school. These are not often taught today, even though kids usually like them. Tell your grandchild the basic story before you read the poem, and then read it aloud with a dramatic flourish, emphasizing the rhythm and the rhyme. Here are some suggestions for narrative poems you can find in any library: "The Wreck of the Hesperus" or "Paul Revere's Ride" by Longfellow, "The Highwayman" by Alfred Noyes, "The Man on the Flying Trapeze" (author unknown), or "Casey at the Bat" by Ernest Lawrence Thayer.

Take an Imaginary Trip Together

Looking at a map of the world, decide together on the perfect destination. Once you've decided where you want to vacation, you can have fun reading about and researching travel arrangements for your destination.

- Check out books from the library and find out everything you'd like to know about your vacation spot. Look for big glossy photo books as well as travel guides.

- Send for free tourist information; you can find addresses online—or simply go directly to a tourist website.

- Read through the travel guides and tourist information, deciding such details as at which hotel you'll stay, what restaurants you'll try, and what attractions and landmarks you'll visit. (You can also do many of these activities online, actually viewing hotel lobbies and guest rooms.)

- Research airline fares. These are sometimes listed in the travel section of the Sunday newspaper or they can be researched online. This activity provides great practice in following directions and reading charts.

- If you've picked a foreign destination, check the currency exchange rate and do a little math to find out how much a soda pop would cost. For added fun, learn a few words in the language of the country you'll be visiting.

Creative Fun

Whenever your grandchild is creating, you get treated to twice the fun—an opportunity to be creative yourself, and an opportunity to marvel at your grandchild's emerging creativity. For many kids, the fun comes from the process of creating, and the end product is merely an added bonus. So if the activity takes a direction you hadn't planned, enjoy the detour.

The following activities are roughly arranged in "toddler-and-up" order; however, older children often enjoy many of the simpler activities.

Paint with Water

WHAT YOU'LL NEED

A bucket of water
Old paintbrushes (house-painting size)

DIRECTIONS

Suggest to your very young grandchild that the two of you "paint" the house or fence. This is an amazingly satisfying activity for a toddler (and a great photo opportunity).

Make Colored Water

WHAT YOU'LL NEED

A bucket of water

Several clear plastic bottles (from dishwashing liquid, etc.)

Food coloring

A funnel (optional, but fun)

<u>DIRECTIONS</u>

Simply add food coloring to bottles of water, close tightly, and shake. Small children like to dump the colored water out, and repeat the activity (sometimes endlessly). You can also do some simple color mixing if your grandchild is interested.

Be sure to explain that the dye may stay on the hands for a while; if that seems to be an upsetting idea, let the child fill the bottle with water. You can add the color, close the lid tightly, and then let the child shake it.

Note: Grandparent and grandchild should wear old clothes.

Cornmeal "Sand" Table

This is a variation of the sand tables once provided in kindergartens.

WHAT YOU'LL NEED

> A grocery carton approximately 18″ × 30″ with three-inch sides
>
> Enough cornmeal to fill the box half full
>
> A plastic drop cloth, an old shower curtain, or a sheet
>
> Assorted small plastic containers

DIRECTIONS

Place your grandchild and the grocery box with cornmeal in the center of the drop cloth. You won't have to explain anything to the child, but you might need to know that it's enormous fun to fill things, dump them out, and so on. A child might also like to make mountains and roads for small cars to drive through.

Note: At the end of playtime, the cornmeal can be dumped into a large plastic garbage bag for next time.

Homemade Play-Clay

<u>WHAT YOU'LL NEED</u>
> ½ cup salt
> 1 cup flour
> ½ teaspoon vinegar
> ¼ cup water
> A few drops of food coloring

Mix all of the ingredients together and knead thoroughly. Get out cookie cutters, a rolling pin, muffin tins, and other sculpting implements and have fun.

Note: Store the clay in the refrigerator. Let it come to room temperature before reusing.

Paint an Aquarium Masterpiece

WHAT YOU'LL NEED

Unlined paper

Crayons

Light blue water (mix a little food coloring with water in a jar)

Paintbrush

With crayons, draw an underwater scene of brightly colored fish and underwater plants. Do not color in the background. Lightly paint the blue water over the whole picture; let it dry, and you'll each have an underwater masterpiece.

Yarn Giants

WHAT YOU'LL NEED

Yarn

An expanse of carpet or concrete to work on (the bigger the area the better!)

DIRECTIONS

Using yarn, make the outline of a really huge person on the floor or driveway. Younger children will need a lot of assistance, and their giant outlines will be relatively simple; older children will want to add every detail.

After the outline is complete, cut pieces of yarn to create facial features, hair (this can become particularly involved when creating a she-giant), striped or polka-dot shirts, shoe-strings, and so on.

Note: You may want to "save" the giant by taking its photo.

Hidden Colors

WHAT YOU'LL NEED

> 6-inch heavy paper square (a cut-up brown paper grocery bag will work)
>
> Crayons
>
> Large safety pins

DIRECTIONS

Completely color in the paper square with various brightly colored crayons. Press as hard as you can. When the paper is completely colored in, cover the whole drawing with black crayon. Use the safety pin to scratch a design on the paper and the hidden colors will show through.

Chalt Art Paperweight

WHAT YOU'LL NEED

Pieces of different colored chalk

Salt

Small glass jars with lids (olive or jelly jars work well)

Butter knife

Small bowl

Funnel (you can make one from paper)
Glue

DIRECTIONS

Pour a mound of salt into the bowl. Scrape the side of a piece of chalk with the knife, letting the scrapings fall into the bowl. Stir with the knife to begin making the "chalt." Continue adding chalk until you like the color you've created.

Using the funnel, pour a small layer of chalt into a jar. Then pour a small layer of plain salt into the jar. Repeat with other colors, alternating with plain salt, and making lots of layers.

When the jar is full, glue on the lid. (You might want to paint the lid first to match the chalt colors.)

Make Your Own Paint

WHAT YOU'LL NEED

Liquid starch
4–6 glass jars (jelly-jar size)
Yellow, red, and blue food coloring
Old pencils

DIRECTIONS

Fill each empty jar about three-fourths full with liquid starch. Add a few drops of food coloring to make one red, one blue, and one yellow jar of paint. Then stir well using the old pencils. If you would like additional colors, mix together the primary colors you've already made.

Note: "Emergency" paintbrushes can be made by using rubber bands to attach sponges to old pencils. What to paint on? Try grocery cartons or paper sacks cut into "canvases."

Printing

WHAT YOU'LL NEED

Paint (you can use the recipe on page 79)

Shallow plastic food containers (like margarine tubs)

Paper (you can cut sheets from paper grocery bags)
or pieces of cloth

Printing implements such as sponges cut into shapes,
spools, nails, or a potato masher. You can also do
vegetable printing by using a design cut into half a
potato or the clean end of carrots, celery, or other
easy-to-cut veggies.

DIRECTIONS

Pour a small amount of paint into the plastic container. Dip
the printing implement into the paint. Lift it out and gently
shake off excess paint. Press the printing tool onto the paper
or cloth canvas and hold briefly. Lift carefully to reveal the
stamped image.

Creating all-over patterns is a satisfying activity. After your grandchild has mastered that skill, try printing an alternating pattern using two printing implements and two different colors.

Note: Use large printed sheets and cloths as wrapping paper. Print on small sheets of folded paper to make matching gift cards.

Beans and More Beans

<u>WHAT YOU'LL NEED</u>

> Assorted packages of dried beans, peas, lentils, and other legumes
>
> Glue
>
> Squares of cardboard cut from grocery cartons (6–8″ is a good size) OR

Discarded items such as cans with smooth edges, old
    saucers, or picture frames
Varnish and brush or clear fingernail polish

<u>DIRECTIONS</u>

Start with a bean border: make a three-inch line of glue,
stop and add beans, then do another section. Next, make
the inside of the picture. You might suggest making the
design one or two colors and the background a third. (Older
children will probably want to draw out a design before
beginning.) Let the mosaic dry thoroughly and then varnish
if you wish.

Older children might also like to mosaic other items (a
more difficult task). When working on a vertical surface,
such as the sides of a can, use only lightweight legumes—
lentils should work well.

Miniature Hats

WHAT YOU'LL NEED

Styrofoam or paper cups
Lightweight cardboard (from cereal boxes, for
    example)
Scissors, glue, pencil
Scraps of cloth, lace, felt, ribbon, yarn, and other
    trims

DIRECTIONS FOR LADIES' HATS

Cut off and discard the top half of a Styrofoam cup. Cut a circle of cardboard about one inch larger in diameter than the cut edge of the cup. Center the cut edge of the cup on the cardboard and glue. This is a basic hat. Decorate with glued-on trim until the hat suits your grandchild's fancy.

Cut off and discard the top half of a paper cup; the bottom half of the cup will be the "cap" portion of the hat. Draw a "bill" of cardboard in the right proportion to the paper cup, and extend the bill so that you have a circular end that fits exactly under the cup. Cut out the base for the hat, and glue it to the cup. The finished form should resemble a baseball cap. Decorate it with your grandchild's favorite team logos.

Fancy Furniture

Note: This is a more-than-one-day activity.

WHAT YOU'LL NEED

An old, ready-to-be-discarded piece of wooden furniture such as an end table or a chair

Sandpaper

Rags
Washable latex paint in a light color (check your
    basement for leftovers)
2 paintbrushes, one for paint and one for varnish
Fine-tipped permanent markers
Paper and pencil
Varnish

<u>DIRECTIONS</u>

Thoroughly sand the piece of furniture. Dust it off, wipe with a damp cloth, and allow it to dry.

Paint the piece of furniture with the latex paint. It will probably take more than one coat. Let each coat dry completely. During the drying time, use the paper and pencil to plan and practice drawing decorations for the furniture. For example, your grandchild might like flowers, rockets, animals, or faces. The two of you could write words and messages or even a little verse.

When the chair has thoroughly dried, make light pencil drawings on the furniture to show where the decorations will be drawn. Go over the pencil lines with markers—the more colors the better! Be sure to add your signatures.

Wait a couple of days and then finish with two or three coats of varnish.

Treasure Box

WHAT YOU'LL NEED

Shiny magazine covers

Scissors

Glue

Any small box with a separate lid (if the box is not a plain color, paint it before you begin the project)

Clear fingernail polish (optional)

<u>DIRECTIONS</u>

Cut the magazine covers into half-inch squares. Work with your grandchild to carefully glue the squares (use the brightest colors) all over the box, leaving a tiny space around the sides of each square. Let it dry thoroughly. To better preserve the box, put a coat or two of clear fingernail polish over the pictures.

Be a Cut-Up

Old magazines offer all kinds of opportunities for creativity. If you don't subscribe to a variety of magazines, you might trade with friends and relatives or ask them to rescue magazines they have set aside for the recycling bin.

Make a Creature from Outer Space

Cut out various body parts from pictures of human beings and combine them in a collage with a variety of inanimate objects. For example, eyes might be pasted onto a cutout of a grapefruit with basketball player arms extending out from it, wheels attached at the bottom, and a VCR perched on top of its head.

Make Paper Chains

Cut colorful pages into strips, staple the ends together to form a ring, link the next ring through the first one, and repeat. Make a chain representing the number of days until a birthday, a holiday, the next time the two of you will get together, or just make chains for decoration.

Make Beads from Brightly Colored Pages

Cut a pennant-shaped triangle about one inch at the wide end and extending about five inches to the point. Put a little glue on the side you don't want to show and carefully roll the triangle around the middle of a toothpick, gluing down the end securely. You've now made a tube-shaped bead. Slide it off the toothpick and make more. String them onto wire or thread to make necklaces or bracelets.

Make Puzzles to Trade with Each Other
Find a colorful magazine picture that can be cut into a square (the bigger the better). Glue the picture onto a same-sized square of cardboard. Using a ruler and a marker, divide your picture into a tic-tac-toe grid of nine squares. Cut out the squares, shuffle, place them inside an envelope, and trade.

Costume Jewelry Dump

If a grandmother has accumulated a drawerful of costume jewelry she'll never wear, a granddaughter might enjoy going through it all and trying it on. But when the fascination with that activity fades, try creating a "jewelry junkyard" by taking all of the jewelry apart.

Kids (boys, too) get a big kick out of dismantling necklaces bead by bead. Provide some egg cartons or small boxes for sorting and separating the beads and jewelry parts into different kinds. Then, when the junkyard is complete, get out some fishing line and create necklaces and bracelets from the various beads. Keep or give as gifts.

Make Greeting Cards
(and a secret plan for their delivery)

WHAT YOU'LL NEED
    Old greeting cards
    Scissors

Glue
White or colored paper
Envelopes
Markers

<u>DIRECTIONS</u>

Start by cutting words and small pictures from old greeting cards. (See the Collecting Fun chapter.) Make new cards by folding and cutting paper to fit into any envelopes you have on hand. Decorate the cards by gluing the cutouts onto the new cards. Kids can also write their own messages or glue on ready-made phrases such as "Happy Birthday." Sign the cards and slide them into envelopes, which can be decorated with additional cutouts.

Your grandchild can then take a card home and "hide" it in a little-used picture book or other out-of-sight place. (Grandparent: Make sure you write down where the card is hidden!) On the special day, call and remind your grandchild about the hidden card.

Wild, Zany, Imaginative Collages
(flat or three-dimensional)

If you keep a box of collage materials on hand, there is no end to the fun the two of you can have creating. Flat collages can be made on squares cut from grocery cartons, while three-dimensional collages can take any size or shape.

Here's a list of materials to get you started: old magazines, catalogs, fliers, and other paper "stuff"; buttons, ribbons, lace, sequins, and other trim from discarded clothes; small hardware items such as screws, washers, and wire; miscellaneous small items like cotton balls, toothpicks, feathers, and shells. *Good quality white glue is a must.*

A fantasy robot, an incredible machine, a dollhouse, a castle, a skyscraper—these are just a few possibilities for three-dimensional collages that can be constructed from castoffs. To the above list of materials, you might add the following: decorating leftovers such as carpet scraps, tiles, and wallpaper; paper party plates and cups; empty cans of all sizes, from tuna to soup to coffee; empty boxes of all sizes, from pudding boxes to grocery cartons; cardboard tubes from bathroom tissue, gift wrap, and paper towels; empty plastic bottles of all sizes; and so on.

Note: In your zeal to participate in the creative process, it's sometimes a good idea to think of yourself as the facilitator or assistant, rather than the designer. Your fun will come from listening to your grandchild's imaginative ideas and helping to implement them.

Thinking Fun

What is more wondrous than watching kids develop brainpower? "How do they *know* that?" we ask in amazement.

It's great fun to play while encouraging those emerging cognitive skills, but it's also important to keep in mind that developmental differences give some children certain skills at one age, while other children—equally bright—may not develop the same skills until much later.

So try out these ideas with this contingency: If it's fun, we play it; if it's not fun, who needs it?

Hey! What's Wrong Here?

Ask your grandchild to take a good look around the room. Send him or her out of the room and make a change. You might move a vase to a different table, for example. Call the child back into the room and ask, "Hey! What's wrong here?" The older the child, the more subtle the changes can be. Children particularly like making minuscule changes and challenging you to find them.

Category Play

DIRECTIONS FOR THE EASIEST VERSION

Name a category and let the child find objects within that category and bring them to you. For example, ask your grandchild to find three things in the house made of wood. Then let the child give you a category. Don't be surprised if very small children give you the same category you gave them.

DIRECTIONS FOR A MEDIUM VERSION

Place a ruler, a pencil, and a wooden spoon on the table. Ask "What category do these all belong in?" To increase the difficulty of this version, see if the child can put the same three items into several categories: things made from wood, things that are long, things that are made in factories.

DIRECTIONS FOR THE HARDEST VERSION

Ask the child to make up a category game by finding three objects for which *you* must determine a category. You may be hard-pressed when an ice cream cone, a pencil, and a bottle of glue are presented for your solution. (These all have one pointy end.) Older kids like to be challenged with this version.

Fantasy Furniture
(a good in-the-car activity)

Propose the following: What would the perfect chair be like? Comfortable, sure. But now, let's get carried away. It could have a refrigerator compartment on the side that would keep your favorite soda chilled, it could have an automatic music selector that would send out music from the built-in speakers to match your mood, it would have a remote control that could . . .

Tables, beds, couches, dressers, desks—dream up the ultimate version of each and share your ideas. Older kids get into this idea with electronics instead of furniture.

Brainteasers

The library has dozens of books filled with these, but here are a few traditional ones to get you started. The fun in brainteasers comes not only in solving them but also in learning them well enough so that you can try them out on someone else.

Problem 1

Mario is always in a hurry. He always ends up wearing one green sock and one red sock. He's got a drawer full of socks, all red and green, but he's in such a hurry that he just pulls out two and puts them on. What's the smallest number of socks Mario would have to take out of his drawer in order to end up with two that match? (*Answer: 3*)

Problem 2
Keisha says she can put her right hand somewhere where her left hand can't touch it. Is that possible? (*Answer: Yes—if she puts her right hand on her left elbow.*)

Problem 3
James has never met you and doesn't know your name, yet he says he can write your name upside down. Is that possible? (*Answer: Yes, he will simply write the words "your name" and turn the paper upside down.*)

Problem 4
Ellen and Carmen say they can read each other's minds. Carmen leaves the room, and Ellen puts three books on a table. She tells you to point to one of the books.

When Carmen comes back into the room, she guesses correctly which book you pointed to. She does it correctly every time. How is that possible? (*Answer: If you pick the book on the left, Ellen calls out "Come back now." If you pick the book on the right Ellen calls "OK," and if you pick the middle book, she calls "All right.")*

What If?
(another good in-the-car activity)

No right answers here, just interesting ones! Take turns coming up with answers for these questions and then make up more for you to try out on each other.

> What if pigs could fly?
> What if mirrors showed how you look on the inside?
> What if French fries made you speak in French?
> What if trees could talk?
> What if people couldn't clap their hands?
> What if pencils didn't have erasers or computers
>   didn't have delete keys?

Size It Up!

WHAT YOU'LL NEED

Pens (not pencils) and paper
A paper lunch sack with the following items inside:
A stick of gum
A quarter
One playing card with a diamond on it
An unsharpened pencil
A dollar bill
A small paper clip

DIRECTIONS

Draw the following items on a piece of paper (without looking in the sack):

- A rectangle the size of a piece of gum
- A circle the size of a quarter
- A diamond the size it appears on a playing card

- A line the length of a new pencil
- A rectangle the size of a dollar bill
- A line the length of a small paper clip

Open the sack and compare your drawings to the objects. See how close you came.

Leave the objects in the sack, and try the activity again the next time the two of you are together to see how much you have improved.

Take Action

What kind of action would each of you take in a hypothetical situation? Present one of the following circumstances with the question "What would you do?" Give your own answer, too. Lots of discussion openers can be found here. After you've tried these, make up more for each other.

- You're on your way to school and you drop an important assignment into a huge mud puddle.

- You need to leave for a birthday party in five minutes. You bought your friend a birthday gift, but you can't find any wrapping paper.

- At night, all the lights go out during a thunderstorm and you can't find the flashlight.

- During the same thunderstorm, you realize you have to get up at 6:30 the next morning, but there's no electricity to run your alarm clock.

- You are trying to make fudge, but it will not harden; it's just sitting in a big puddle in the bottom of the pot.

- You are walking down the street to a friend's house by yourself when you see an enormous strange dog.

- You stand up in school to give your book report, and all of a sudden you can't remember what the book was about.

- Your aunt asks you to hold your baby cousin for ten minutes while she takes a quick shower. The baby starts screaming.

- You go to a friend's house for dinner and you absolutely hate everything that's being served.

- You need a book from the top shelf of a bookcase that you cannot reach even while standing on a chair.

And the Answer Is…1089

Grandchildren who are taught this trick are guaranteed to try it out several times on everyone they know—including you.

<u>DIRECTIONS</u>

❶ Write down three single numbers in sequence, counting backward (876, for example). ❷ Now write the same numbers counting forward (678). ❸ Subtract the second number from the first number. ❹ Reverse that number. ❺ Add the answer to #3 to the answer to #4.

Amazingly, the number you get will always be 1089!

To the Store Without a List

Make an estimate of how many grocery items each of you thinks you could remember without looking at a list. Start with a list of twelve items (vary the number depending on the age of the child) and then use each of the following memory aids to recall the list.

- *Story Time*. Devise a little story that mentions all the objects. For example: "The *pudding* tasted like *carrots* so I traded it for *pumpkin*-flavored *potato chips* to eat with my *butter* and *jelly whole wheat bread* sandwich which I *squashed* flat when I slipped on some *oil* while I was trying to lift ten pounds of *potatoes*, a *turkey*, and a giant *watermelon* all at once!"

- *Tippy Tower*. Make a mental picture of yourself creating a tower of the objects you need to buy. You'd probably put the bag of potatoes on the bottom, and the potato chips on the top. Construct it carefully, and you'll be able to remember every item.

Make Maps

Drawing paper and pencils are all you need for a variety of mapmaking activities. Have your grandchild try some of the following (listed in approximate order of difficulty).

- Take a good look around the room. Then go into a second room and try to draw a map of the first room by showing where each large piece of furniture, each window, and each door is located.

- Draw a blueprint of one floor of the house. Try for reasonable proportions and include doorways, halls, steps, and so on.

- Draw a map of your grandchild's or your block. Show the position of houses and buildings, street(s), driveways, streetlights, fire hydrants, and stop signs.

- Draw a map of the best route from your house to someplace nearby, such as a school or a grocery store.

- Draw a map of your state and then add the ones that surround it. Drawing a map of the entire United States freehand is an ambitious challenge.

- Draw a map of the world showing the continents.

- Draw a map of the universe showing the planets.

Estimate

It's always fun to make guesses, and that's what estimating really is. The more your grandkids try, the better they'll become at making estimates. Try estimating and then checking out the actual answers for the following, and then make up more of your own things to estimate.

- The length of your shoestrings
- The number of shelves in the refrigerator
- The length of time it takes to fill a gallon container of water from the faucet
- The number of pieces of macaroni it takes to fill a one-cup measure
- The circumference of a broom (or an egg or a dinner plate)
- The number of pages in your dictionary

Learn the Words for
Really Huge Numbers

Everybody knows that a one followed by a zero is ten, a one followed by two zeros is one hundred, and a one followed by three zeros is one thousand. Try learning the names for one followed by the number of zeros listed below.

Six zeros: a million
Nine zeros: a billion
Twelve zeros: a trillion
Fifteen zeros: a quadrillion
Eighteen zeros: a quintillion
Twenty-one zeros: a sextillion
Twenty-four zeros: a septillion
Twenty-seven zeros: an octillion
Thirty zeros: a nonillion

Analogies

You don't have to be gearing up for the SAT's to have fun with analogies. Try these for starters:

Cat is to kitten as dog is to _____ (puppy).

Pen is to ink as brush is to _____ (paint).

Foot is to shoe as hand is to _____ (glove).

Boat is to water as plane is to _____ (air).

Coffee is to cup as soup is to _____ (bowl).

Baseball is to bat as tennis ball is to _____ (racket).

Man is to boy as woman is to _____ (girl).

Month is to year as hour is to _____ (day).

Word is to sentence as letter is to _____ (word).

For even more analogy fun, come up with some new ones together. Your original analogies can be more subjective, such as the following:

Scary movies are to _____ as _____ are to me.

Uncle Bill is to Kevin as Uncle Stan is to _____.

Grandma is to motorcycles as Kim is to _____.

No "Yesses" and No "Nos"

Here's a sneaky way to increase the level of conversation. Give your grandchild ten nickels with the instructions to never say the words "yes" or "no." Throughout the day, every time your grandchild slips, take away a nickel.

For example, the answer to the question "Do you want brussels sprouts for dinner?" is not "No," but something like "I would never eat brussels sprouts for dinner."

To increase the fun, put ten nickels in your own pocket; you have to pay out a nickel every time you say "yes" or "no," as well. *Caution*: Your grandchild will think up devious ways to trap you.

Music Fun

Children respond naturally to music. Rhythm and melody speak to them, and they answer back with movement and sounds of their own. And while children are delighted to hear their favorite tunes over and over, they're also incredibly open to new musical experiences. Try some of the activities in this chapter and find the joy of music together.

Homemade Instruments

Generally speaking, it's true that the smaller the child, the bigger the satisfaction he or she will get from simple, homemade instruments. For example, banging two pot lids together with music playing in the background is a rewarding activity for grandkids who have not even reached their first birthdays. Here are a variety of possibilities for kids who are a little older.

- Shaking two plastic-coated paper plates stapled together with a variety of small metal objects inside—or even unpopped popcorn—makes a great sound. Aluminum-foil pie plates are even more nicely noisy. (Older kids might like to make them for younger ones—and try them out in the process.)

- Stretch rubber bands around a variety of objects, including chair backs, empty coffee cans, or sturdy boxes, and you'll be rewarded with some interesting strumming and plucking possibilities.

- Gluing two paper cups together with a handful of rice or macaroni inside results in a pleasant-sounding shaker. Other shakers can be made by putting a variety of objects inside small jars.

- Wrap two large building blocks in sandpaper and rub them together for a pleasant "whooshing" sound.

- Slap two wooden rulers against each other.

- Punch several holes in a cardboard bathroom tissue tube and cover one end with waxed paper. You can tape the waxed paper down or use a rubber band. Hum into the open end for an interesting sound.

- On a towel, line up a bunch of glass tumblers. Use a pitcher to pour different amounts of water into the glasses. Use a pencil to tap the rims of the glasses and determine the pitch. Arrange the glasses in order (according to how high or low they sound). Try to play a little song.

Note: Even older kids get into this activity because of the challenge of manipulating the glasses to get the sounds exactly right.

Color to Music

WHAT YOU'LL NEED

Paper
Crayons
A radio or a CD player with a variety of discs

Put on some music and color the way that particular music makes you feel: excited, calm, jumpy, sad. What colors does the music sound like? Talk about how the music makes you feel. Change the music every few minutes.

That's Dancing!

C'mon. There's no one here but the two of you. What more joyful experience can there possibly be than going with the flow of the music and dancing around the room with your grandchild. But do it quickly—inhibitions take over quite early and if you wait even a little while, you will have missed your chance.

Play "Name That Tune"

Once a child has established his or her favorites and has a little repertoire of recognizable songs ("Happy Birthday," or "Twinkle, Twinkle, Little Star," for example), try humming a few notes and see how many it takes before the tune is recognized. Older children might enjoy singing the notes for you to guess.

Note: This is not an activity for the tone-deaf grandparent unless there happens to be a piano or a keyboard in the house.

Dinner Music

Be brave. Put your grandchild in charge of dinner music at your house.

Marching Bands

Everyone loves the flair of a marching band. Look for opportunities to hear them, perhaps at a community festival or parade. You might also find out when your local high school band rehearses; you can climb up into the bleachers and enjoy a nearly private performance without the noise of the Friday night football crowd.

The Great American Musical

Introduce your grandchild to the concept of musical theater. Start by telling the basic story of an appropriate show such as *Oliver* or *The Sound of Music*. Next, you might want to get a copy of the video from the library and watch all or parts of it together. If you have a recording of the musical, loan it to your grandchild. And don't forget to demonstrate on every possible occasion how many of the songs you know by heart.

Community theaters sometimes present outdoor musicals in the summertime for little or no cost.

Note: If you happen to be an opera lover, you can try the same approach by reading aloud a children's book that tells the story of an opera (perhaps *Hansel and Gretel* by Humperdinck) and then playing one or two brief selections from it.

Great Classical Recordings for Kids

If you're interested in sharing your appreciation of classical music with your grandchild, the following are good introductory pieces. Rather than trying to listen to the entire recording, offer just a taste of the music. Most of these recordings can be checked out from the library.

- "Peter and the Wolf " (Prokofiev)
- "Young People's Guide to the Orchestra" (Britten)
- "Wellington's Victory March" (Beethoven)
- "Carnival of the Animals" (Saint-Saëns)
- "Symphony #101, 'The Clock'" (Haydn)

Free Concerts

Most cities offer a variety of free concerts, perhaps presented by community bands or symphony orchestras, particularly during the summer, and most high school and college bands don't charge admission to their concerts.

Prepare a child for a concert by explaining concert manners and by checking out a library book that has pictures of different musical instruments. Try to arrive early in order to sit near the front. This way you can see the orchestra members prepare, and you will have an opportunity to identify the instruments.

If your grandchild has never been to a concert—or is very young—it is perfectly appropriate to attend the concert for only one or two selections and then leave quietly between pieces. You'll know when it's time to stay for an entire concert!

Award for Valor

If your grandchild is a teenager, you might suggest watching MTV together and rating the music videos. You might surprise each other. And you'll probably increase that surprise by sharing some of the music you listened to when you were your grandchild's age.

Writing Fun

Seeing our own words on paper is satisfying, and if the process of creating those words is fun, it's an added bonus.

The entertainment value of writing went up about 1000 percent with the advent of the computer. The energy kids once had to expend laboriously printing out block letters or forming devilishly complicated cursive ones can now be put to better use in the actual creative process. And the professional look of the finished product is a bonus when using a computer.

Using the computer or not, writing together is a great activity for building relationships. As teachers often discover, experiencing the thoughts of a child in written form can provide incredible, never-before-noticed aspects of the child's personality, feelings, and ideas.

And just think what your grandchild might discover about you!

Write a Picture of Each Other

Sure, it might be fun to draw a picture of each other, but a word picture is entertaining, too—and revealing. Do some research and observation before writing. Measure and weigh each other. Be precise in describing hair and eye color. Compare your skin tones by looking in the mirror. Describe your outfits in detail. Get barefoot and describe each other's toes! The idea is to pretend that you are *writing* a photo—stick to describing how each of you look in as much detail as possible.

Turn Yourselves into Acronyms

Unlike the previous activity, the description in these acronyms is intended to reveal personality and character.

<u>DIRECTIONS</u>

Grandchild: Write whatever name you call your grandparent, placing one letter at the beginning of each line on your paper. Make each one a capital letter. *Grandparent:* Do the same with your grandchild's name.

Fill in each line horizontally with a characteristic, habit, saying, like or dislike, positive quality, or other description of your subject. Start each one with the first letter in that line.

You might have to come up with a few neutral first words to get you both started. Notice the use of "just," "really," and "yet to" in the following example.

J ust learned to swim
E specially likes to ride his bike
F orgets to be mad for long
F ast at tying his shoes
R eally knows the multiplication tables
E ager to turn 10
Y et to turn down a chocolate cake

Note: You might need to explain that an acronym is a word formed from the initials of other words. Scuba is a good example: Self Contained Underwater Breathing Apparatus.

Family Newsletter

A perfect grandparent/grandchild activity is creating a family newsletter—it provides an opportunity to view family events from two different perspectives. While a younger

---

child might enjoy simply adding drawings to your handwritten words, older kids will enjoy pulling out all the stops with a computer edition of the newsletter fortified with professional-style graphics. The newsletter can be snail mailed, E-mailed, or distributed at family gatherings.

Starting Letters, Ending Letters

Try writing super-long sentences in which each word must start with the last letter of the previous word. Here are two fun examples:

> "Four red ducks sat together reading great tennis stories."

> "Willie expected dessert Tuesday, yet the enormous sweet tart that Tess served didn't taste exactly yummy."

Make sure your sentences make sense. This activity is great thinking fun and a great way to get kids to spend a little time with the dictionary.

Write Reviews

First, check out the "Read Reviews" idea in the Reading Fun chapter. After reading lots of reviews together, try your hands at writing some. You might want to try writing reviews of children's books, TV shows, movies, songs, or restaurants. Start with a reminder that reviews usually have two parts: the first usually gives a general objective overview, while the second often gives the reviewer's opinion. After you have written reviews, you might want to "publish" them by offering to post your reviews of children's books at the library or mailing positive restaurant reviews to your favorite places to eat.

Family Crossword Puzzle

Create a large grid for your puzzle. Don't worry about making a pattern like they do in the newspaper, but make sure the words intersect frequently. Number the beginning of each word, and write corresponding clues like "Month in which Matt was born" and "Uncle Ollie's favorite dessert." Don't forget to include an answer key.

It might be fun to make copies of your puzzle and distribute them at your next family gathering.

Dear Famous Person

Writing letters to sports figures, TV stars, book authors, government officials, and other people in the spotlight helps connect kids with the world. You might want to discuss the fact that, as a general rule, the more famous the recipient, the less likely the chances are of receiving a response. With that understood, go ahead and write those letters. Here are a few hints:

- Many addresses can be found online or with the help of the research department of your local library.

- Start the letter by briefly describing who you are.

- Don't worry too much about your grandchild's spelling, but point out that people like to see their own names spelled correctly.

- Make the point of your letter as specific as possible: "Last week on TV I saw that game with the Yankees where you hit three home runs. Wow!" or "I think we have to come up with a way to give teachers more money so they won't quit."

- Limit your letter to one page.

- Thank the recipient for taking the time to read your letter.

- Including a self-addressed stamped envelope might increase the chances of a response.

Doggy Diaries
(also works for cats, gerbils, and other household pets)

WHAT YOU'LL NEED
    A small notepad
    Pen or pencil

PREPARATION
Pose this question to your grandchild: What if the family dog could talk? What would he say about what he did today or what he thinks about other members of the family?

<u>DIRECTIONS</u>

Start a doggy diary. Very small children can dictate their ideas to a grandparent. Date the diary and write down each day's entry. The following are a few fun idea starters:

- Think about the "who, what, where, when, and why" of your dog's day. Who did he play with? What did he eat? Where did he hang out? When did you come home? Why did he get in trouble?

- What did your dog see, hear, smell, taste, and feel?

- What does your dog think about each member of the family?

- What does your dog dream about?

- What do you think your dog wishes for?

- What doesn't your dog like?

Write a Two-Person Play

Putting together a little dialogue is fun, especially if the two of you can practice and "perform" your play for other members of the family.

First, decide who your characters will be. You can just be yourselves, you can play each other, you could be famous people, or you can even make up fantasy characters. Then think of a problem for your play. Here are some examples:

- A grandchild tells a grandmother that her new camera has been lost.

- You are two lost hikers who argue about which is the best way to get back home.

- A grandfather tells his grandchild he has found a lost dog; the grandchild wants the grandfather to keep it at his house, but he doesn't want to.

- You are two actors in a movie who are arguing about whose name should appear first in the credits.

- You are two classmates who were assigned a team project; you are arguing over who should draw and who should write.

- You are two garbage collectors who argue about which of them should get to keep the chair the rich people threw out.

- A grandchild tells a grandparent that he or she wants to _____, but the grandparent says _____.

As you write the play, make sure the problem gets a little complicated; then come up with a logical (or funny) solution. If you're actually going to present your play, wear name tags saying who you are supposed to be. Costumes are fun, too. Grandchildren can dress as their grandparents, and vice versa when appropriate.

Get Perfect!

Each of you writes the descriptions of the following "perfects" (and any other "perfects" you want to add). Compare answers.

- Describe the perfect outfit.
- Describe what you would be doing that would make a perfect day.
- Describe the perfect vacation.
- Describe the perfect lunch.
- Describe the perfect friend.

Take-Your-Turn Stories

You begin by writing or typing the first few lines of a fantasy story. Then your grandchild dictates (or writes/types) the next few lines. The story doesn't have to be finished in one day; it can be picked up and added to whenever the mood suits. It might also become an E-mail project. Here are some story-starters you might like to try.

- Nicki seemed to be an ordinary kid; however, Tasha discovered the truth about her one rainy afternoon.

- For three nights in a row Ben heard a strange thumping sound that seemed to be coming from the attic.

- When the zookeeper came to work that morning, she could not understand how the orangutan and the lion had changed places.

- The Smiths were happy about their new house until unusual things started to happen.

- If the teacher knew about the seven bats hovering just outside the classroom window, she wasn't talking about it.

- The snow was pink, a definite rose pink, but the weather-man didn't seem to have any explanations.

- Alonzo told Sam to meet him behind the apartment building right after school and to bring the biggest box he could find.

- Angela wasn't sure if she was scared or just excited the morning she found out that being invisible wasn't impossible after all.

- One morning Bidi, the troll, decided to challenge the giant on the hill because the giant would never let Bidi . . .

Mystery Family Tree

This is a good activity to keep both of you occupied while waiting for a holiday or family celebration to begin.

<u>WHAT YOU'LL NEED</u>

>A large sheet of poster board (or you could use the back of a large sheet of gift wrapping paper)
>Green construction paper
>Ruler, scissors, pencil, pen, glue
>Brown marker
>Scrap paper

<u>DIRECTIONS</u>

Start by brainstorming—come up with as many funny and entertaining family stories as the two of you can remember. For example, stories like "the time Grandma dropped the Thanksgiving turkey," "the day Uncle Matt lost his shoes in a snowdrift," "the time no one could find Samantha because she was sleeping under the bed," "the birthday party that had the wrong time on the invitation," and so on. Jot down (or type) each memory on a piece of scrap paper and check over the way it's written. Does anything need to be explained more clearly?

Using green construction paper, cut out the same number of leaves as you have stories (15–20 is a good number). Make the leaves big enough to write your stories on.

Now for the mystery part: instead of using real names in the stories, use a made-up name as you write the stories on the leaves. You might want to use a ruler so that you can write your stories in straight lines, or if you are typing, you could just print the stories onto light green paper.

Then, using the brown marker, draw a large tree on the poster board. Glue on the leaves so that they are nearly touching but not overlapping any of your words.

Display your Family Tree in an obvious spot. Then stand back and watch the fun as everyone discovers just who they are on the mystery tree.

Patchwork Words

WHAT YOU'LL NEED

Old magazines

Plain paper

Scissors, glue

DIRECTIONS FOR VERSION ONE

Find magazine headlines and advertisements with large, colorful letters. Cut out individual letters (cut a box around them rather than trying to cut out the actual letters themselves). Glue a message on paper using the letters you found. Deliver the message anonymously!

DIRECTIONS FOR VERSION TWO

Instead of cutting out letters, cut out whole words.

Rhyme Time...Forever

Writing the world's longest rhyming poem can be a continuing activity, one that could last for many months, or even years, to be worked on whenever the spirit moves either of you.

<u>DIRECTIONS</u>

Explain that your poem is going to be written in couplets (two rhyming lines). You should start the poem with something general and simple. For example:

> It's good to have fun
> In the rain or the sun.

Your grandchild could add the next couplet. Something like:

> When it's sunny, I always like
> To take a walk or ride my bike.

Followed by:

> On a day that's wet and foggy
> I play inside with my new doggy.

OR

> When it's rainy, icky, quite dark
> I stay inside and train my aardvark.

Hang the beginning of the poem somewhere tall, but out of the way, like a closet door. As you add couplets, you may need to tape more paper onto the first sheet.

Note: Checking out a rhyming dictionary will add to the fun of this activity. Your grandchild will have a great time looking through it, and he or she will discover that "second-guesser" rhymes with "tongue depressor."

Legal Graffiti

After years of telling your children that writing on the walls was out, why not make it "in" for your grandchildren.

If you have a wall in the basement, attic, or garage that needs a bit of character, why not turn it into the "Great Wall of Thoughts and Ideas." Let a young grandchild begin with a handprint and be sure to add the date. Then from time to time, you and your grandchild can make a stop at the writing wall. Add doodles, notes about what's been happening in your lives, what you've been thinking about, questions, little poems, notes about what you've read or seen at the movies, notes about friends, relatives, and pets. Add dates every so often.

This activity is kind of like a growth chart, except that instead of a size record, it's a writing record.

Silly Fun

No explanation needed here; some-times it's great fun to do something just for the silliness of it, like making weird faces at each other or speaking in Pig Latin. So have some fun with these silly activities.

Tasting Contest

WHAT YOU'LL NEED

A dozen or so small (bathroom size) paper cups

A blindfold

Spoons

Various liquid-y foods or condiments, such as mustard, catsup, salad dressings, taco sauce, lemon, orange, and other juices, soda pop, mayonnaise, horseradish sauce, peanut butter, jelly, honey, and so on

PREPARATION

Secretly put a small amount of five or six of these ingredients into separate paper cups. Blindfold the taster, your grandchild.

DIRECTIONS

Hand your grandchild a spoon and a cup. Give instructions to "taste and guess." Keep track of how many correct guesses are made. Then you get a turn.

Note: Older kids like to try this activity using only various brands and flavors of soft drinks.

Sure Bets

Explain that all of these bets have trick answers. Encourage guessing before you demonstrate "the catch." Help your grandchild to understand the trick well enough to try it out on someone else (probably a parent), and then have a practice run.

BETS:

A. I bet I can show you an object that you will have never seen before and you will never see again.

B. I bet I can drop some sugar into a cup of coffee without getting the sugar wet.

C. I bet I can stand two inches away from you and you won't be able to touch me.

D. I bet I can put two pieces of candy under two hats, eat the candy, and then put the candy back under the hats.

E. I bet I can put a dime under a quarter without touching the quarter.

F. I bet I can put a paper napkin where everyone can see it but me.

AND THE CATCH IS . . .

A. Take a walnut, crack it open, and eat the nut. (You'll never see *that* nut again.)

B. Fill a cup with dry coffee, and then dump in the sugar.

C. You stand on one side of a closed door, and your grandchild is on the other side.

D. Eat the candy. Put both hats on your head. (The candy *is* under the hats.)

E. Put a quarter on the table; tape the dime under the table directly below.

F. Put the paper napkin on your head.

Pun Fun

What's interesting about playing with puns is discovering at what age kids seem to "get it." Understanding plays on words is a kind of abstract thinking, and that skill develops at different ages in different kids. So, try these out from time to time and watch to see when the lightbulb switches on. There's another way to know if your grandchild gets it—remember that another word for a pun is a "groaner."

Libraries stock books filled with puns, but to get you started, here are a few written especially for kids. They're called "Hugo Definitions."

Avenue: "Lucky, lucky me!" Hugo said, "I avenue video game."

Cartoon: His mother said it was irritating to drive Hugo anywhere because he kept singing dreadfully awful cartoons.

Daisy: Hugo skips out so often that his teachers are really surprised on daisies at school.

Historian: Hugo's big lie is obviously ridiculous, but that's historian he's sticking with it.

Juicy: Juicy the size of those watermelons in Hugo's garden?

Laziness: His mother complained that Hugo never accomplishes anything; he just laziness bed and watches TV.

Miniature: Hugo's mother complains that he always disappears when it's time to do chores, even teeny tiny ones. "One miniature here and one minute you're gone," she said.

Sofa: Hugo was testing out the new living room furniture. "Sofa so good," he said.

Thick: Hugo's mother kept telling him to exercise, and she warned him to stop eating so much candy. "You'll get thick to your stomach," she said.

Wade: Hugo said he'd dive off the high board, but he wanted to wade a few minutes before he tried it.

Blibbering

In this guessing game, the word "blibber" always means to do a specific thing. The guesser must guess what the blibberer did by asking yes or no questions. Before you begin, decide on a time limit or a certain number of questions. A game might go like this:

> The blibberer says, "Last weekend I blibbered. What did I do?"
> The guesser asks, "Did you blibber outside?"
> Blibberer: "I blibbered outside."
> Guesser: "Did you blibber at night?

Play continues with the guesser trying to find out just what the blibbering was. If either player neglects to say some form of the word "blibber" in his or her question or answer, that player is automatically out.

Stuffed People

Have a great time seeing your old clothes live again by creating a special somebody or a whole group of porch sitters.

<u>WHAT YOU'LL NEED</u>

>Old clothes, shoes, and accessories (rescue these from the Goodwill bag)
>Old gloves or disposable ones
>Lots of old newspapers
>Something to be used for the heads: old pillowcases, small trash bags, hats, masks, yarn, etc.
>Safety pins
>Markers

<u>DIRECTIONS</u>

On the floor, lay out your person's outfit. For this example, we're making a boy, but women in dresses can be made using panty hose or tights.

Start by stuffing his shirt with wadded up newspapers. (It might be fun to explain to your grandchild what the expression "stuffed shirt" means.) Next, stuff his pants, leaving some newspaper hanging out the bottom of the legs, and then stuff his shirttails securely into his pants. Put a belt through the loops. Stuff the newspaper from the bottoms of the pants legs into his shoes and tie them securely.

Now add hands. Carefully stuff each glove with newspaper. If you're using clear disposable gloves, you might want to stuff them with rags instead. Next, make the head: stuff an old pillowcase or a small white plastic trash bag with paper and then add his features with a marker. You'll probably have to use safety pins to get his head to stay on (attach it to the shirt collar).

To make your person as real looking as possible, top him off with a very large hat. Other possibilities include yarn or an old mop for hair or a mask for the face.

Note: Stuffed people like to sit in places where they can watch the action.

Tongue Twisters

Sure, everyone knows "Peter Piper picked a peck of pickled peppers" and "She sells seashells by the seashore," but what about "Six silly snakes slithered slowly southward" or "Mister Minster's mystery mirror mirrored Mister Minster's mysterious mother"?

Books listing tongue twisters are available in the library, and learning to say them flawlessly is fun. But it's also fun to make them up. Here are some guidelines:

- The best initial sounds include B, F, G, M, P, R, and S.
- Use at least four words with the same beginning consonant (you might want to tell kids that poets call this alliteration).
- The sentence should make some sense. (And who will be the judge of that?)

Can Walkers

All you need for stilt-type fun is a little rope and four empty coffee cans (the large ones).

DIRECTIONS

First, punch a quarter-inch hole next to the rim on the bottom of the can, and then punch another hole on the opposite side. Tie a large knot at one end of the rope and thread it from the inside of the can through one of the holes. Pull the rope through until the knot stops, and then thread it through the other hole, going from the outside to the inside of the can. Tie a knot in the rope on the inside of the can at the place when you can stand up on the can and hold on to the rope without bending your elbow.

Repeat with another can. Then make a second set so that you and your grandchild each have your own pair of cans. Now you are set: put one foot on each can, hold onto the rope, and take robot steps on your new stilts.

Backward Be

Just for fun, fill a couple of minutes or an entire day with the following backward activities.

Eat dessert before dinner

Eat meals in this order: dinner, afternoon snack, lunch, breakfast

Talk backward. "Fun having I'm." "Puzzle new a bought I."

Walk, run, or hop backward.

Put on as many of your clothes backward as possible.

Read a children's book starting from the last page and ending with the first page.

Write your name backward.

Count backward from 10 or 100.

Learn a Clever Party Trick I

WHAT YOU'LL NEED

Six paper cups
A marker
Water

DIRECTIONS

Line up six cups and number them. Fill cups 3, 4, and 5 half full of water. Here's the challenge: put the cups in alternating order (water, no water, water, no water, water, no water) by moving only one cup.

(How it works: Simply pick up cup 4 and pour the contents into cup 1.)

Learn a Clever Party Trick II

Fit through a piece of paper!

WHAT YOU'LL NEED

    A piece of notebook or copy paper
    Scissors

DIRECTIONS

Fold the paper in half (either way). Cut long slits in the paper about an inch apart starting with the folded side, alternating with the unfolded side, and ending with the folded side. Next, cut the fold but start at the second slit and end at the next to the last slit. Open the paper up, and you'll have a huge hole to step through.

Ludicrous Lyrics

Decide on an easy-to-sing, familiar song such as "Twinkle, Twinkle, Little Star." Decide who or what your lyrics will be about. If your family is planning a gathering soon, you might like to write lyrics about your relatives! Write new lyrics that have the same number of syllables as the song. Try to use some rhyme if you can fit it in.

Here are a couple of examples:

Row, row, row your boat
Sleep, sleep, Uncle Neal
Gently down the stream
Sleep as thunder roars
Merrily, merrily, merrily, merrily
Leaking roof, flooding streets, broken sewer
Life is but a dream.
Uncle Neal just snores.

Twinkle, twinkle, little star
Grandma Betsy, you're so sweet

How I wonder what you are
Always baking us a treat
Up above the world so high
You don't make us eat our peas
Like a diamond in the sky
Brussels sprouts or even beets
Twinkle, twinkle, little star
Grandma Betsy, you're so sweet.

Make lots of copies of the lyrics. Pass them out at the next family gathering and encourage everyone to join in the singing.

Get Moving

Roll down a hill, do the wheelbarrow together, slither like a snake, walk like an elephant, pantomime a window washer, jump and hop, do somersaults. Make an obstacle course out of boxes, chairs, and small tables and time your-selves to see how fast you can make it around the course.

Spend a Million Dollars

Question: What are the differences between how you and your grandchild would spend a million dollars if it suddenly fell into your lap?

OK, you've just won the money, so each of you should privately make a list of how you'd spend the money. (You may have to do a few reality checks on your grandchild's estimate of how much things would cost.) Compare lists.

Yes, it's a silly endeavor but a great conversation starter, and you'll probably learn something about each other.

The Great Theme Park Extravaganza

Anybody can take a grandchild to a theme park; not every-one can design one. Here's a new way to spend a rainy afternoon. On a huge sheet of paper (you can use lots of paper taped together on the back, if necessary), make a plan for an incredibly silly amusement park. Think of a theme and a name like "Worlds of Cheese" or "Plastic Land." Then think up rides and attractions to go with the theme. Map out where the rides will be, write little descriptions, and draw them if you can. Plan where the concession stands will be located and what kind of theme food they'll sell.

OK, maybe not as much fun as actually riding a roller coaster—but lots more imaginative.

And Lots More Fun

. . . Like going out and about together to discover the world through your grandchild's eyes (even if that world is only the other side of the street).

. . . Like working together and appreciating the very special kind of camaraderie that comes from tackling a job as a team.

. . . Like celebrating together because, after all, every day you spend with your grandchild should be a cause for celebration.

Going Out and About

Getting out with your grandchild is a great treat for both of you. You get the fun of some one-on-one time and your grandchild gets the fun of being the entire reason for the outing.

If kids are old enough, they sometimes enjoy planning an expedition. But, especially with younger children, be ready to go with the flow. For example, if you purposely planned an outing so that you would walk by a fire station, but you're halfway there and your grandchild is fascinated with workers repairing a broken streetlight, watching that operation is now the purpose of your walk. Go with it!

Most of the following suggestions cost nothing or nearly nothing. So, out you go!

- Walk around the block and talk about what you see. Look for animals and count how many you see. Look at how many different kinds of mailboxes or address numbers or front doors people have. Watch people working: a mailman, someone changing a tire, someone gardening, and stop to talk when it seems right. Remember that your grandchild might like to ride a trike, push a doll buggy, get pulled in a wagon, push teddy bears in a stroller, skate, or skip.

- Drive (or take a bus) to a nearby location and walk around, particularly if you can easily access an area with stores and businesses different from the ones where your grandchild lives. If you're coming from a suburban area, it's fun to walk around a business district and check out traffic lights and parking meters and shop windows. Listen to honking horns and music coming from people's cars. Ride an elevator in a big building and then look down from the top floor. Look at the building directory to find out what kinds of offices are in the building.

    If your grandchild lives in the city, drive out to the country and walk along a road. Listen to the quiet or listen for birds and try to imitate their calls. See how many kinds of grasses and plants you can find. Examine the fences to see how they were made.

- Go to a construction site where a house is being built. Pull up a piece of ground (out of everyone's way) and watch the action for a while.

- Find out if any nearby factories give tours—it doesn't matter what they manufacture, kids will simply enjoy the adventure.

- Take a ride to the recycler and sort out what you brought.

- Take a ride to the Goodwill store and leave some donated items. Go inside and see what kinds of things they sell.

- Pack up anything that can't be recycled or donated and take it to the dump. Look at the different piles of junk, such as enormous stacks of tires. Talk to someone who works there about what happens to all of that stuff.

- Go for a bus ride and see what you can see. Let your grandchild purchase the tickets and hand them to the driver. Get off somewhere if it looks interesting. You can come back to where you started if you have no other destination.

- Visit city parks not just for the playground equipment but also for promoting (and teaching the manners of) the fascinating activity of people watching.

- Go on impromptu picnics. A sandwich, an apple, and a bottle of water tucked into a bag make a satisfactory lunch for a park bench, a country road, or even the backyard. (And speaking of the backyard, that's the perfect spot for a little one's first overnight camp-out, if you're so inclined.)

- Make a list of what you need at the hardware store; while you're there, walk up and down the aisles looking for interesting stuff.

- When weather permits, do your produce shopping at an open air market. Talk about the variety of produce. See if there's anything either of you would like to try.

- Watch a sporting event. Amateur ones, as well as youth events, are often free to the public. Young children enjoy watching older kids play fast-moving games like soccer.

- Check out art museums; they sometimes have free admission days. Limit the visit to five minutes for each year the child is old, for example, half an hour is plenty of time for a six-year-old. Look at brightly colored paintings, sculpture, and works featuring children and/or animals.

- Go to an ethnic festival. Held in many cities as well as rural areas, these events provide wonderful opportunities for exposing your grandchild to a variety of cultures.

- Go to a concert (see chapter on fun with music).

- Take a stroll though an outdoor art fair. You'll get an opportunity to enjoy the fresh air and to talk to the artists.

Working Together

Very little children enjoy serving as a grandparent's assistant in nearly any around-the-house task. Helping to dust, to polish, to prepare meals, to clean up afterward, to put clothes into the washer, to rake leaves—all of these activities become fun when grandchild and grandparent are partners in the activity. Remember to assign small tasks one at a time, and to give lots of positive reinforcement.

Often, for older grandchildren, "help me out here" somehow gets translated as "perform slave labor." So, in order for more grown-up grandchildren to have fun helping a grandparent, the work must be truly meaningful. Try some of the following ideas.

You'll find a grandchild makes a great companion for the following activities:

- Sorting through that box of old photographs, especially if they get to see hysterically funny snapshots of a parent. Keep in mind that your grandchild may be the only individual on earth interested in seeing home movies of your 1973 trip to Yellowstone.

- Cleaning closets: Look for items to place in a "dress-up bag" for younger kids. For older kids you may actually have a "retro" item they'll be crazy over. (These are also the same grandkids who will tell you frankly what's just too out-of-style for you to be wearing at all.)

- Book or knickknack dusting—if you hide sticks of gum or coins on the shelves for a little reward. Vary the amount from time to time, and never tell how much or what you've hidden!

- Learning more about the computer. No one will make a better instructor than a grandchild incredulous at your lack of computer savvy.

- Gardening, especially when an appropriate size plot is designated for that child alone to care for.

- Volunteering. Look for organizations that will accept the two of you as partners. Try food pantries and recycling centers.

Celebrating

Add to the fun of family celebrations by helping your grand-children prepare some of the following:

- Placemats, napkin holders, and place cards. Make funny place cards by cutting out various bodies from magazines and topping them with snapshots of family members' heads.

- A skit or play for everyone's entertainment (see "Writing Fun"), a poem to recite (see "Reading Fun"), a party trick to perform (see "Silly Fun"), or a few funny lyrics to sing (see "Silly Fun").

- Cookies or a cake made well ahead of time and frozen in secret to be revealed on the big day.

- A treasure hunt complete with clues on a treasure map the two of you create.

Celebrate Offbeat Holidays and Commemorations

Check the library for *Chase's Annual Events* (McGraw-Hill) or a similar publication that will provide you with literally thousands of events you and your grandchild can commemorate just for fun. Here are a few ideas.

- January 18 is officially "Pooh Day." Give a party for Winnie the Pooh. Serve refreshments (honey sandwiches) and read a couple of favorite Pooh stories.

- February is Potato Lovers Month. Create a homemade Mr. Potato Head by using toothpicks and vegetable parts. While you're working, nibble on hot-from-the-oven French fries—a bag of frozen ones makes this easy. And don't forget to try different kinds of seasonings on top.

- March 11 is Johnny Appleseed Day. Plant a tree in his honor.

- For April Fool's Day, provide your grandchildren with a repertoire of appropriate tricks, saving one that you plan to use on them yourself. A favorite: replace the icing in sandwich cookies with toothpaste.

- May (Mother's Day): The first Saturday in the month could become "the official make a present for Mom day" (with your help, of course).

- June (Father's Day): The first Saturday in the month could become "the official make a present for Dad day" (with your help, of course).

- July 20 is the anniversary of the first walk on the moon (1969). Tell your grandchild what you remember about that day.

- August. Make up your own holiday!

- September 28 is National Good Neighbor Day. Find a neighbor who could use some cheering up, some lawn work, or some brownies.

- October 25 is Pablo Picasso's birthday. Check out a few books showing his Cubist work and celebrate by "painting like Picasso."

- November 16 is World Food Day. Collect canned goods and deliver them to a food pantry.

- December 26 is National Whiner's Day. You know where to go with that!

   And finally:

- A truly memorable celebration: Ask your grandchildren to help you prepare a party you are giving that evening for "very special guests." Ask them to help you dust, set the table, prepare the refreshments, arrange flowers, or hang decorations. Thank them profusely for their help. Then send them outside to ring the doorbell; when you answer the door, explain that *they* are the special guests. Have a wonderful evening!